vagrant (one) in thin air

Karen Garthe

with tt

SPUYTEN DUYVIL
NEW YORK CITY

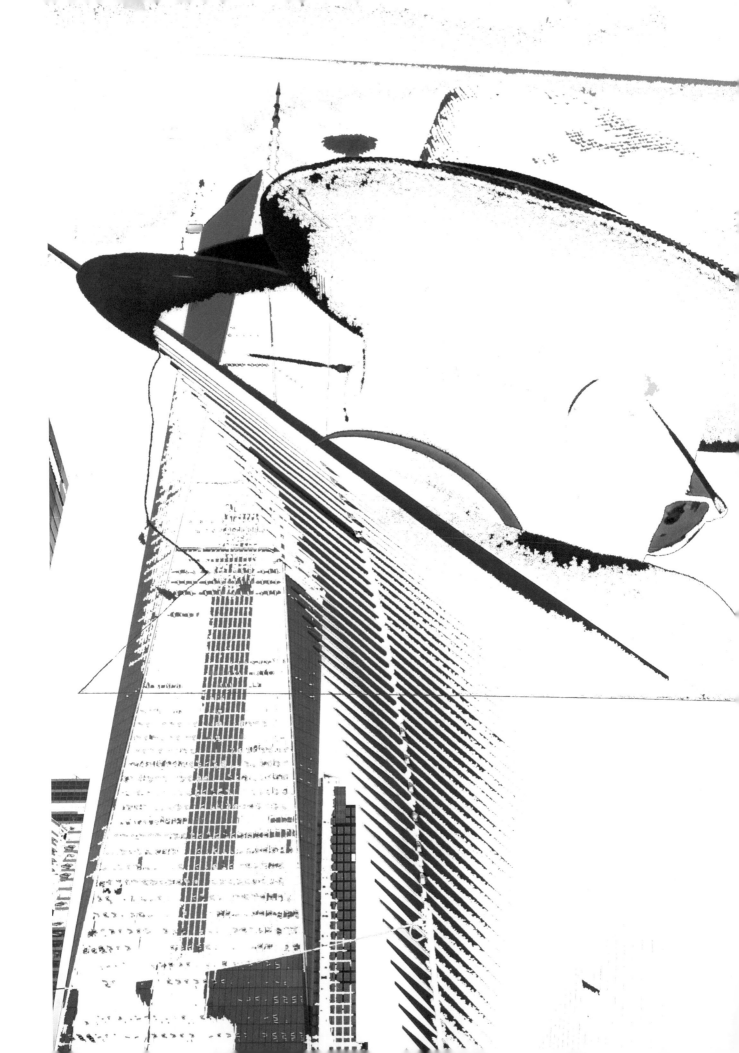

vagrant one in thin air
fathom trinket rummaging parabolas
drift kissing the circus of panic you step in
the wound
shrine filigree

flyball over the moat
Well, there you go   shimmering

for friends of years

Where is the thunder

When will it rain?

The Swan, Baudelaire

Go

smoke on the porch

away from Sugar, her Desires

Yawning   waving the poles...joints and elbow lamp

flicka wands chasing the heels of the game

formulas of deceit yearn forward

on the face of it they've done so well for themselves

hooping zeros, driving

moons

whose stomachs are empty, whose cold whites besmirch

skiing cross country

scribbling the earth "*1928 after one war*

and before another speeds"

the country of Longing, the state of Have

are the haunt of all philosophy

it's getting awfully achy dreadful

sorrow

Clementine. not to hope is forbidden

the truck's parked at the fence

Sal Hepatica, cigarettes and cowboy coffee

heels (*as in louses*) spur the posy papered wall

buzzing critters delirium outside

not to mention a million hot frogs wet

the vistas we need

a SHELTER poETry *of old women, terrible accidents in* The Somewhere

whole crowd standstill   in a downpour

pressing

shelter

pressing the wrap-around dark's old growth rings close

how long can we breathe in here.

how long can we keep our telepathy cheek to cheek?

by now a thousand times over we could have bought that crazed

beautiful house by now

by now

we could have endowed the whole family ruptured and haunting

forest primeval

glowing so   *you shield your eyes*

and wince

SPEED   *dying by its own   quiver*

like fire consumed and consuming

f*lowering*   as in Handsome, Valiant   sweet*of*Heart

& way out on a limb, then, in the *forest primeval* hovering all the spongy maladroit

But   NOW   bumping   the   ferry   I   am

gripping

hot coins to cross   let my luggage pitch in drift

the Old Women

are at **coasting distance**

keeping clot remove

Clementine, say what

Open palm
what happened   what's left

of this
fly by swirling
pinnacle transcendence, this
Whom of persons' radar that the waltzing flowers have reached
their very highest
coldest
zone   triple flagged and egged on
to what known purpose but the most common errand
waltzing *is*
flowers ***still are***
The most trustworthy beautiful blood wound *my heart rolls down my breast*

carry on forthwith, let's face it
we know so many helpless things

Herding, shaping the planet rings . . . a foghorn,
            a destabilizing violin   *that Procol Harem startChord* conversation
                                regarding empire
                    regarding **cruel space**
heart is gold and hard as gold

the end of the rainbow you are
                            loud as atom split
chopping wood for a new Damn Yankee terrace
your own mother carefully minding her own business
keeping
out of it
still
                    you're thrilling
focused that way tragedy strikes

Wealth of Nations

walking Margaret to The Shed &
Grande Chartreuse

~*invitation to the sweet pea*

cut   n'twirled in cellophane   island of scentless, therefore *pointless lilac*
          &
     snapdragons 20 a bunch   2 Apples of Eden 7 dollars
                    7
          mystical number of completion

~*the good life*

                              making sense
                              in friendship
                              making sense
                              palliative
for the dying hero of the good life who doesn't want to leave, who is calling his good life over the fields
          (meantime let's continue... our   eggfluff
     and
                              potatoes convene little alps on platters
                    cube Cezanne
          French villages clamor *Marseilles!   Nantes !   Lyon!*

          Dearest *Paris, The Wealth of Nations*

~saddle-up

We are processing down Leonard now, walking

saddled-up desertions   more than a few

tears

of Gotham myst

vaguely now, remotely now   *just where is the child's lunch withheld   ?*

wherefore some **rural hospital ?**

thru the fuzz of bearded Last Testosterone in the $10,000 dollar crystal dress

comes Liberty LeadingThePeople   *nous sommes arrivé*

~The Shed   HE YEARNS TO BE SHOT (FILMED UP CLOSE

braids row down his side face while shewolfs fury   wolfs the vast starry barge of her

aurora roundup

of rubber hoses   old barn wood whiffs

authentic *Last Chance Texaco*

her   Extravaganza   Bomb

her sudsy ululation's Icelandic shiver   *she bourées*

her wealth

her weal

~& Grande Chartreuse

Toujours   thousand turnips
                vierge milk and our   green/yello
Chartreuse midnight matin   prayer without end   secret heart of the world's

                                suffrage
                                language enraptured bone

Except for bells and coughing only the clock tick talks,
says they've given up all they have they have to become

        light pins in snow dark   chaînes of roses,

                                A tooth of sun on the floor
crazy   from combat in solitude   in   prayer

                                moonlight whitens the table sheer
                        hapless harp of moonlight

Luminous Severence

slim   sharp   Clip of Conference afternoon

huddled in nasal codes, a wedding band combo **To**

the company *pied-à-terre*

YOURS

TRULY, it is

absolutely

*kra*ss as it sounds

yet persists

here on The **R**ocks of **U**tmost

TRULY *YOU need that job* & we need a couple of sweet **J**ust **L**oaves we can carry off

like babes   to that cave a few short

blocks away

*we'll jettison all **T**erms of **S**ervice*

underhanded history   the stew of souls

we'll keep

violence sly, keep our upsweep

CAN DO appetite

but hey. . .say you make a wrong turn and ***you lose***   *in luminous severance*

the shiny knuckle of **O**rdinary **D**ay

and you suddenly face the mirror straight on

a desperado seeing   himself

rapt

Labor omnia
vincit

Virg. 1. Georg

Lunette Halfmoon Ho*rror*   sunrise

causing birds to silence

Big BOOT DOWN THE STAIRS TO where are my elders

Mentors

Revving-up

Hope full sight

far   as   I   ca n   tell

The body landed **Here**

in its tortures   its lone throng in

The Great Vocal Recess's wire shut orbits H*ere*

where violence has really come

hulking

front and center

at the top of the stairs   a dragon scaled with martyr

smear and tars of avenue

filly Chablis

in the armchair of franchise by the catalog drop table

loophole

pulldown   who's worth listening to. . .the ocean of star fish

grappling

devouring

soft oysters. . .our science *data Onward*

      we're off! To Overstock Brothers, then

      rude Mr. Barleycorn, then

some   filly   Chablis   selfie   witching   the   warehouse

where **Old Minerva's standing**

her owl quaint in the corner

convenes all ghosts

stocking every pattern of our replacement here

in the armchair

of franchise

Sunrise Road

flyspecks of panoramic

Self   in   The   Valley

climate melancholia at your heels

the louche dunes. . .look at them windsweep parabolic repentance

your confessed moving on   *blazing*

just running through people

like Frankenstein

propelled

so helplessly

forced to life

both bone gentle and crushing

bumper car glee bruising wholeness

keying the cars in the lot

dont hogwash me

I   already   forgot   The   Suburbs   high   flat   tar   hot   railroad   crossed

the extra space for living here but no room to breathe

I   *willingly* relinquish carglide   random gunsmoke random   sunrisesunset Anglo named streets

that Split-Level-Now longing

for

some shed-in-a-box space to curl up and *pill alone*   (yes

I'lll   miss   us jockeying curves and swerving many-mansion-splendor

the State Fair my bath was   the lamb I grew

so *fragile I grew*

chronically **dizzy**

You said you had my back

I hoped we could   steam out the wrinkles   **really could**

silk down Sunrise Road

Pinch me out

A *blue*

poseur

murmuring her own

driving her own

disappearance   in simulation   I saw

f ootprints retrace the labyrinth

step by step back

to the

beginning

*P*inch me out as starlit

clamor

Love

doubt Love, Love

conjured, Mesmered

spells

made

my train of shabby gown   *a*   sugar

pelt

to swing down risible aisles

you can't just walk off like that

across the hardwood gleaming the whole web of life You're my buoyant

cupping antic flames under the rain sheets, the eave's sodden bundles

you can't just walk off. . .

I'll gladly play that bubbly roller rink organ for you, pump the thrillway

in glycerin smooth

accord

we can take on much younger voices, we can chatter straight thru but

you can't just walk off. . .

you have such lank & Lovely Winter Hair

I know you know how to call the purple, call us back on fire

Clementine (I, I, I)

blaspheme gasps

the hot core of mercy

is all

up

hill

Clementine,   *your crabbed talent*

for

sideways

is perfectly sly

&I

am trenchant with memory

serene even though   I've lost my train

my purple foothills and my language-bright

crocuses in snow

I establish half scholar

. . .half fay

imagining   you've eased downhill

more tranquil now

that is

If I've not **made**

a ruin

this tired afternoon

Coleridge

What if you slept

And what if

In your sleep

You dreamed

And what if

In your dream

You went to heaven

And there picked a strange and beautiful flower

And what if

When you awoke

You had that flower in your hand

Ah, what then?

Swan song

Garbo Interlude

the stretched-out hands are alight in the darkness like an old town

Mr. Cogito, Zbignew Herbert

Mink Boy

afraid of The Cold   not crisp air but *low fellowship*
made her wall part roses part
mud

fear
the Holiday Gift Mart tinsel zinged
exclamatory snow's little rockets of solitude

shot
her mink boy
walked and talked

sprinting *forever sleepless*
wee hours crouched over
the drive

thrum barges
pushed
the age

Palette rose

I rest in

unkempt

attars

twiddling fingers 10 kissings in air

rendered mulberry pink   so *bound in*

laughter amongst the images

Alone in my corner **b*ef*ell**

solace **b*ef*ell**   reaching my hands in   the sorest

rose of opening illness

tantamount's pinkest

salmon-colored coruscations effervesce

Vast Absence twilight harbors   The gray blue East River

Slips

450 East 52nd Street

boy.

...er if you did go to Marbella?

...not know what to decide on this ...
...again with Cecile to Sardinia, b...
...t for me, so I am not going. I...
...vitation from a lady in the Sout...
...willing to stay quiet, but time ...
...rk out, I suppose I leave.

...also has asked me to go for two ...
...   The boat is too small and I he...
...ns living on sleeping pills. We ...
...all just have to see how I feel.

...am trying to tell you, I guess, ...
...ee you later, if you are there. ...
...a line (I plan to leave New York...
...ess will be

    c/o Princess Anja Chervachidze
    Villa Soulico
    Roquebrune

What she meant *was the gift of chit-chat*

between the poles   EXUberance   DESpair

posting

*fa*ncy sorrow whose breezed head tilts

throat rings bared to the rail

Tolstoy's *Alpha*

Femme

Fa*tale* way she does and does not care. . .

and **So I Ask a great favor of a queen**   cradling the phone's

handful of riot

that anything so beautiful should ever come to me

The O*ld* S*oul Garbo's*   Anna Karenina **has**

lost her cattle

lost her honest peasants and high*Noon* feasts

s t i l l Anna sugars her buttons, her **k**nock **k**nock bustle

& *especial glacé* falls to the neckline

her sledge across the tundra of Late Desire

the dropdead canary pecking at her heels and the atlas of all kin-pouncing chimes

Rome Suite

coifs of underwater

language I need

for the help

I need a thong of craft, a barque

a pirogue

Turtle Fountain

if there's a word over Love

over&above The Brains of Language

in that rule-burnt kiln of Latin, say, *amas*   (by-with-from

dative shards

of choiring Greek Boys   say I hear you

vertiginously

running the cobblestone thresh

beheading the lilies of beatitude

Sanctuary HereBy "a few Jews for Hitler"   . . .**what Mussolini said**

a mere 5 hours from now

in military time

the racket gulls   honeycomb gut folio and pendant amphorae

sway

monumentality Here

vehiculum flayed Pasolini

Hit him & Hit him again

over & over &

above

Magliana

His trumpet   *hectoring*

  SourBell

  Droll Capo

  filching

  this part of Rome collapsing

  balconies

  ragging laundry

And there he is *hectoring*

keening

shot within

And bull's eye here I sit

     stabbing

my pen in Spartan luxury

*of those worn **dirty graces***

cluttering the rails

fins to water   wings to

caterwauling steel

belts

punched

squeezed

in curdled mortars in chewed cement

the shoes of the river's quiet crime

repose

wrought in plain sight

with   indefatigable grace they **hang**

on

iron beams

Splendor Slaves

Giordano's *petticoat* **rusts**Splendor

*S*laves stick to palazzo walls   cisterns gush

down

under Rome's blood moon we begin

beautiful daughters in softness   we adjourn

to death's sinecure

and sacramental Floor of Pity   **We Are** *the brides of*

your kill

*J*unk

bracelet Coliseums for sale on migrant chains, the avalanche crushed Apennine Hotel

red Rome artichokes

wreathe Giordano Bruno now constitutes bronze, bronze of **so much light-bearing P***ity*

the   street   singer's   trilling

green parrots lavish

blue   underwing

the Ferrari takes to

7 Whole Hills

the apartment stays palest green on top of the hill

cloud punch prevails   adjusting

louvers on the terrace

petting Blue Madonnas **we left Detroit to herself** dilapidating

here we have our white grape

vines cascading bygones and furthermore

you

so cunningly. . . so ineluctably

treacherous

hmm...we completely share how we get that

(we have bad dreams since we sleep too long

big gulls shuffle the split cork roof

the Medusa of thick swooning vines   here relax, **have another**

Here's

our Eden   piping sulfurous Last Things

alert and so savagely mistrusting

the metal blackout blinds   the gate crashed down

on the pawnshop we left

Detroit dilapidating

day in day out

there' not much to say here in our Eden carriage of prestige *rowing the Aventine*

The bus load, the cocktail complex breeze

sanctus unguentum burning the eyes

scar travertine's sworn vertigo

my run thru fear a roundabout

singing

bowl of light

hooded crows balance the tops

of new growth cypress, fierce wind R*enaming*

Every Beloved Thing

He was so nearly here with me today was **perfect bread**

and sun

and salt

on mouthfuls of silver

all a' glistening

Then the dark Twister her pique beat back

so

I'm checking the Timetables right now

departures   finalties keep us Sane

Rome

close and so familiar   The flogged stones

reports of sun breaking out everywhere **Rome is**

so close and so familiar, she may as well be brushing my hair

she got up early just to cut

down

her best   tree **for her exclusive** *stoking rights to fire*

THEN   she rained and rained and rained

flaying her covenant ossuary her skull roll rigged down tender views

she cut and stood

her own

shibboleth   part she ran

rioting   gutters'   split   clay

betrayal   hags   and   wink

HEAVY DRINKING OF THE MERCHANT CLASS AND PRINCES

malt moon

pageant fragrant tuberose

night so drunk resounds *I'll steal along your Keep Flame,* lick your delicate

            burn edge,

          Your True Knife

Pronounce "rings of hard failure"

the stone flute's breathy   tolling superskills & selection-without-end

                        bulk

                  surmise of surmise

                 so

      flammable Asking For Anything

flies, it flies

thinking **surely** *by now*   *by now* **The Thinker has awakened**

I GREW UP ON CHICKEN-PECKED EARTH

the goat head cooked long and slow was father's sublimity   *eyes like gessoes*

               Mar*ble*   Alabas*ter*   Gyp*sum*

           (the goat regarded you as the head cooked long and slow

Now, which exotic thread, sub-zero lap dance stares into

   the project?

     which thread to fear. . .Russian divers or their tanks

       when they blow up blow *toward, blow into* The Body

               I grew up on

       chicken-pecked earth

Hecate was present
and that other woman looking backward –

tearful, holding onto the rail.

I saw it futurally

The Farewell Stairway, Barbara Guest

the faces of so many

In the arms of *what-to-think, how to rudder paw*

Babylon's wicket

make a mercy blanket warm

& re-soul babble breath

the Faces of so many small believing animals

are picking their way to this

calculus

of wild vines

picking their way from the dirge trumpet shake down they're finding the

Mercy

Flare

softens everything

dusky hams the chilblains and bunts

raw devils of exposure

The AIDS Monkey

I should have taken your picture 93bl*ue-eye years*

stemming a chair   glamorous as pampas tousling wind

you were

waiting on the dog-child

ever-barking and pierced she was

cutting

her   scars

Prison of green *lawnette*   porch patch   room we parked in

singing

small cadences flung to the sideboard   afternoon

sun mottled

that priceless   Dresden monkey

tipping his hat, glistening

eternal, the Jade Mountain clambered its crags   in the shadow's

Rollickingdeath mask   *of a Mother/Daughter blood-curdling soliloquy*

still We Performed The Dream cardinal and first

First, my yello-spray tulle sequins ran the scales and haloed vertebrae

we tore all the sheets into bandages   every supper

a hazmat portfolio: cold chicken   gallon Chablis

the Endless Field of Stuff   of salves   and   minaret   *perfumes*

glacial Dolomite, powdered *noh*

Your unconditional forgiveness diamond,

Your hammered gold

thatInsane

caved-in   pale Dresden

Monkey (we *named The AIDS Monkey*

his **hat**

thrust out for change

chatting thru the ether
we're not the
only racket

frills the wreck

steeple storming

shape
notes
barking

for each other over the river
current tongs
we're set
side by side

to meld
& bank and stream

Le Massage

handing down the spine   my very own upPeriscope   *Lookout*

Apogee

nobody tenders near

your clinical sweep a Zamboni polishing ice so skaters glide

sure-footed

smooth

how   apply   for this access

to this Blue Hour's *OnceUponaTimetherewas* an Ancient part of Paris called Le Marais

(nowadays Upscale Global Everywhere)   We were strolling, me and my new friend

our last moments on

Earth

Together Girls

in that blue hour of still-embodied persons

we were waltzing *I mean* **really   really waltzing**

handing down my spine you called out *our Radio of Last Days,* the superNatural radio

((you know, that

one

m e s s a g e s

all the booksellers *dans le Quay, gifting each their sunrise*, their deep stall fluttering

spine of stairs down to the Seine

that way

lost persons flock in the body, flock forever in the muscles and blood

you scrolled &   levied

to Martine

balm in Gilead

on a hillside in Crete

Even dead and gone, love labors

the   Arrow   in   your   side   fletched

the wound

instructs

Heal thyself

this low-growth merciful herb expels the arrow

*our **eye-to-eye marveling***

iris rings

the hillside in Crete's stable hay

the matted- sleep-on-years

of decencies   you won't regret turning the leaves

bleeding here   on the hillside

Study Spain

The grass and gushing maples are

The *Casanovas* of good sugar   *you know, so many split their trunks*

to fold

over envy. . .

over there one leaf glitters   unnaturally tinsel darts

a way into the great cave of Casanova's

gush

(. . .there's One Shag Dead One   A *Lone Gargantuan* Lob Pine

axel of the maples spreading . . .one leaf glittering unnaturally

is the black*R*ed

tip   off   summers   end   *stretched pleasures of coolness, the mounding clouds. . .*

how Casanova

cheated death by simply getting into a taxi

grit pock/Vector magic   roots gathering the end-bones and

centuries as study Spain, *LISTEN:*   **Fernando has left us, he disappears**

he will remain in being for many

knowledge and passion and the creative dimension

we remain

a little more orphans in a trance of extinction we are in

The farewell

All of us

movING shelter

midst trees   **gushing Fo*rward* to** the Casanova s of   good   sugar

Caravansary   ripe

tent hoists

Duende

her rhythmic death bath

soothing **The Infanta in toweling mink**, *in her*

Great Goya shrug of Personal Best. . .

A defenseless

revolutionary hilltop is kissing the castle   kissing the Trinity thru stark

alienation   terminals

gilt Apocalypse

the fatal foreman's tools of access throttling, brandishing

tusks of   great mammals

knit

under tarp

&

The Oracle of The **Mouth**

Nectars

shipwrecked people once called souls chamber under the floor

BAWLMER FOF

a needle poises   her sliver glints in the dark

just *turn . . .swerve*   b*ank emotional water. . .*there Is

an open-wide   in   **the   kelp   forest   Miracle Marine**

the DedEnds are needling   one's about to sew her

peacock-eye surveillance

the other rips coupons of suburban frizz

and the tallest longest needling spins so fast she warps

a simulacrum

of primal voluptuousness, a fecund Willendorf seduction

but *we have our service roads*   *mash gates in place*

to save our creatures and every miniscule

Our Big Bears Coaxed Out by

Balmy Zephyrs

WE STILL HAVE *OUR SLY service*   *roads AND mash gates*

for

quiet realms and naming

Now such DedEnds cavort under the microscope They master the sky's colicky

Bulk

A sly terminus bouquet

stems *constellate and*

broider . . .

E*scape*

        *we've got ser*vice roads and the gates are in place
    to perplex the Needle Stewards' hoke black brim

            we stashed our terminals
    our   landmark   forests   siren
          Harbinger and Perplex
      SWerve & **Vanish**
   like a magical city under attack
sharp   down the   service   road
          drive home

even then **RoseRed**

we knew a dream

        in a dream

neither snow nor rose we billowed

the range

ridge and field a luscious

plot,

involved that Man-worn Theosopher

we shared

        his Perfect English Benign

        Rose we were

        our own child

& when we spoke a *kind of speech gold*

beauty in the air made candy of

        sense and extra

        sense wind

        our braid

You may be weaker than the whole world but you are always stronger than yourself.
Let me send my power against my power. So what if I die.

Love's Work, Gillian Rose

*Maybe she'll come tonight on **her zephyr that ends with a***

wedding

ravishing down the page
Or maybe our girl is right now

newly gentled, breathing through the star on her forehead

((I could never have endured
the poison unless cupid flourished the tree rooted upside down in the sky

((and yes: maybe she'll come tonight and yes. . . yes
we can change the color of our eyes
together
to see
that   mothlike tawny miniature,
Benjamin's Angel of History
My AngeLofDeath   a   lite   tin   urn   in   shade we'll see   torrents
in the great bear hug of evil

One whole year under a false sun

*But   with   The*S*un's remembrance*

In Hebrew

In Hebrew 'ruach'
is spirit, wind
the verb's to hover
back & forth

In Syriac the same
word means to brood
but any old context's
sexual course

Babylon's creation myth
gods are really at it
Marduk "ruaches' Tiamat
(mortal foe)

Till she exceeds
the Hindenburg, then
his arrow splits
Tiamat in two

Half of her
he pitched & made firmament
half he flung
& laid the ancient world

Plain Mary gets 'ruached'
by ear, fluting
Gabriel buzzed
her half

To death
assigned the sons
& many
fear nots

Breed
in glassy wind
& hover
still

Trick Monkey

I fell North and bounce
    Fill my capes with lead
To beat the wind
    I live in sunset
Colors and cold wind
    Sit in ruined amphitheaters
One character too far
    The moon loses her light
The stars their radiance
    In this marvelous presence
I enter the Big Top
    I live in the sunset
*Now, not yet. . .**tip my hat***
    When the reds come out

THE FAULTLESS CAMPAIGN OF A GATHERER
I made this sumptuous lookout

under gray mouse, under scotch fawn

matt groundcover

the croft woods prescient, limned

as a blithe **yello rose**

tucked in crucial green

leafed as Cassel's Fairy Tale Trail

a dyed-in-the-wool manger

to the Narnia wards of old

oak spirit and phenomenal love

not another place like it is so *faced*

borne and listening

With gratitude to the editors of publications in which some of these poems have appeared

Caliban Online

Exquisite Corpse

Flag & Void

HERE

Lana Turner, A Journal of Poetry and Opinion

Unearthed Online Literary Journal

Thank you to Victor Gunsalus for the image facing *Clementine* and to Christopher Ludgate for the image facing *Quiet Crime*.

ASSOATE

CPSIA information can be obtained
at www.ICGtesting.com
Printed in the USA
BVHW021227040521
605599BV00007B/22